Ants

Debbie and Brendan Gallagher

 **Marshall Cavendish**
Benchmark
New York

Library of Congress Cataloging-in-Publication Data

Gallagher, Debbie, 1969–
   Ants / Debbie Gallagher.
     p. cm. — (Mighty minibeasts)
Includes index.
Summary: "Discusses the features, habitat, food, life cycle, living habits, and unique behaviors of ants"—Provided by publisher.
ISBN 978-1-60870-542-9
1. Ants—Juvenile literature. I. Title.
QL568.F7 G35 2012
595.79/6—dc22
                              2010037191

First published in 2011 by
MACMILLAN EDUCATION AUSTRALIA PTY LTD
15–19 Claremont Street, South Yarra 3141

Visit our website at www.macmillan.com.au or go directly to www.macmillanlibrary.com.au

Associated companies and representatives throughout the world.

Copyright Text © Debbie Gallagher 2011

Publisher: Carmel Heron
Commissioning Editor: Niki Horin
Managing Editor: Vanessa Lanaway
Editor: Tim Clarke
Proofreader: Gill Owens
Designer: Kerri Wilson (cover and text)
Page layout: Domenic Lauricella
Photo research: Legendimages
Illustrator: Gaston Vanzet
Production Controller: Vanessa Johnson

Printed in China

Acknowledgments
The authors and the publisher are grateful to the following for permission to reproduce copyright material:

Front cover photograph: A weaver ant © Dreamstime.com/ Liewwk.
Photographs courtesy of: ANTPhoto.com.au/Jim Frazier, 15 (top), /Otto Rogge, 15 (bottom); Auscape/Patrice Olivier-BIOS, 14 (bottom); Dreamstime.com/Cobretti, 21 (center above), /Hakoar, 21 (top), /Liewwk, 1, 9 (top), /Linda Macpherson, 20, 21 (center), /Naturamagallery, 22, /Mike Nettleship, 21 (bottom), /Pardeep08, 21 (center below), /Ryszard, 13, /Unteroffizier, 6; Getty Images/Mark Moffett, 27; iStockphoto/Vladimir Davydov, 11 (top left), /Colin Ewington, 11 (bottom center); Minden Pictures/Satoshi Kuribayashi, 23, /Mark Moffett, 8 (bottom), 9 (bottom); National Geographic Stock/Minden Pictures/Mark Moffett, 16; Natural Sciences Image Library, Peter E. Smith, 11 (bottom right); Photolibrary/James L Amos, 12, /NBenvie, 30, /Russell Bruden, 24, /Scott Camazine, 18, /Michael J Doolittle, 28, /Juniors Bildarchiv, 14 (top), Patrick Landmann, 25, /Wayne Lynch, 10 (top), /Stephen P Parker, 19, /SPL, 11 (bottom left), /SPL/Goetgheluck Pascal, 8 (top), 7; Pixmac/Liewwk, 11 (top right), /Shane Partridge, 10 (bottom), /timur1970, 29; Shutterstock/orionmystery@flickr, 5, /Ljupco Smokovski, 3, 4, 17.

While every care has been taken to trace and acknowledge copyright, the publisher tenders their apologies for any accidental infringement where copyright has proved untraceable. They would be pleased to come to a suitable arrangement with the rightful owner in each case.

135642

Contents

When a word is printed in **bold**, you can look up its meaning in the Glossary on page 31.

Mighty Minibeasts

Minibeasts are small animals, such as flies and spiders. Although they are small, minibeasts are a mighty collection of animals. They belong to three animal groups: arthropods, molluscs, or annelids.

	Animal Group		
	Arthropods	**Molluscs**	**Annelids**
Main Feature	Arthropods have an outer skeleton and a body that is divided into sections.	Most molluscs have a soft body that is not divided into sections.	Annelids have a soft body made up of many sections.
Examples of Minibeasts	Insects, such as ants, beetles, cockroaches, and wasps **Arachnids**, such as spiders and scorpions Centipedes and millipedes	Snails and slugs	Earthworms Leeches

More than three-quarters of all animals are minibeasts!

Ants

Ants are minibeasts. They belong to the arthropod group of animals. This means they have an outer skeleton and a body divided into sections. Ants are a type of insect.

Ants are closely related to bees and wasps.

What Do Ants Look Like?

Ants have a body divided into three main parts. These parts are the head, the **thorax**, and the **abdomen**. They have six legs, which are joined to the thorax.

Ants have a long body with a narrow waist.

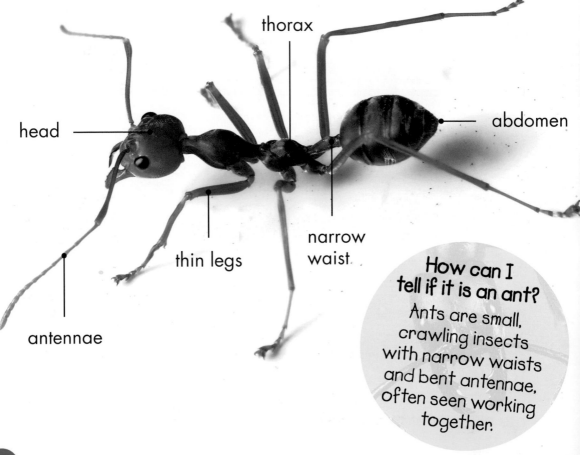

thorax

head

abdomen

thin legs

narrow waist

antennae

How can I tell if it is an ant?
Ants are small, crawling insects with narrow waists and bent antennae, often seen working together.

Ants have two strong jaws, called mandibles, and two **antennae** on their head. They also have two compound eyes, which are made up of lots of tiny eyes.

Ants use their special features to sense the world around them.

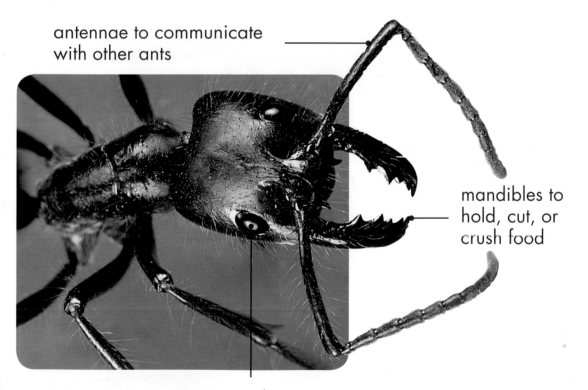

antennae to communicate with other ants

mandibles to hold, cut, or crush food

compound eyes to see well

Different Types of Ants

There are more than 12,000 different **species** of ants. The largest ants can grow up to 1½ inches (4 centimeters) long. The smallest ants can be as tiny as ¹⁄₂₄ inch (1 millimeter) long.

The largest ants in the world are sometimes called dinosaur ants.

1½ inches (4 centimeters)

Some of the smallest ants would fit on the tip of a pencil.

¹⁄₂₄ inch (1 millimeter)

Ants come in many colors, from black and brown to red and orange. Different ants have different abilities.

Trap-jaw ants can shut their jaws more than two thousand times faster than humans can blink.

attacking ant   carpenter ant

Carpenter ants can kill attacking ants by exploding sticky yellow glue over them.

sticky yellow glue

Where in the World Are Ants Found?

Ants can be found all around the world, except in Antarctica, Greenland, and Iceland.

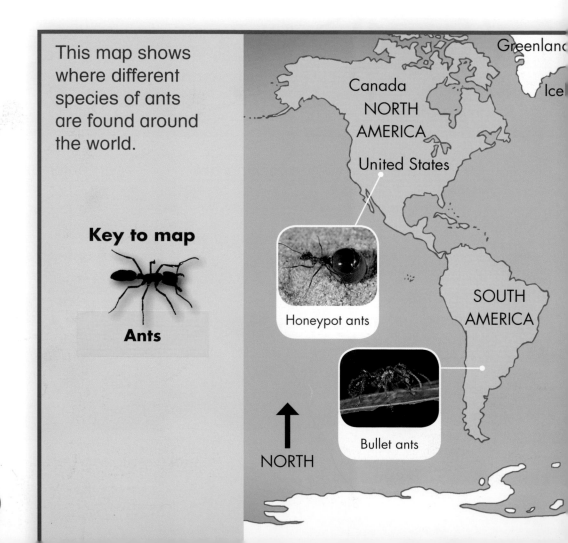

This map shows where different species of ants are found around the world.

Key to map

Ants

Greenland

Ice

Canada

NORTH AMERICA

United States

Honeypot ants

SOUTH AMERICA

Bullet ants

NORTH

They do not live in places that are extremely cold.
Ants can be found on most islands.

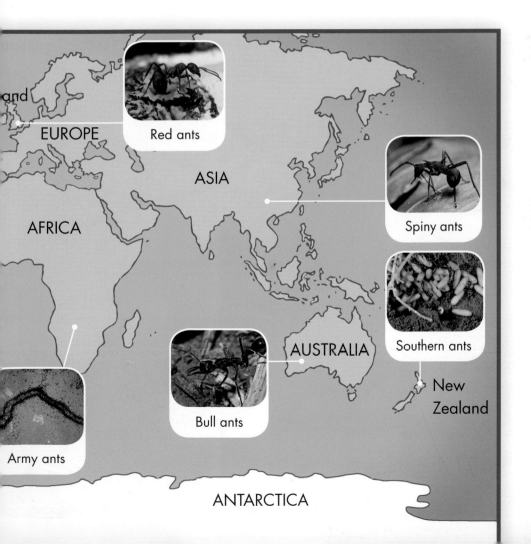

and

EUROPE

Red ants

ASIA

Spiny ants

AFRICA

Southern ants

AUSTRALIA

New
Zealand

Bull ants

Army ants

ANTARCTICA

Habitats of Ants

Ants live in nearly all types of **habitats**. They live in deserts, grasslands, and forests. Ants also live in places where people live, such as towns and cities.

Long-legged ants live in desert habitats.

More types of ants live in rain forests than in any other habitat. Rain forests have lots of food and places for ants to live.

Trees in the rain forest have large leaves, which leaf-cutter ants use to make their food.

Life Cycles of Ants

A life cycle diagram shows the stages of an ant's life, from newborn to adult.

1. A new queen ant leaves her nest to **mate** with a male ant. The queen then makes a new nest and lays her eggs.

4. After about two weeks, adult ants hatch out of the cocoons.

Most ants are worker ants. They live for only a few weeks or months. Some queen ants can live for several years.

larvae

2. After about two weeks, **larvae** (say *lar-vee*) hatch from the eggs. The larvae eat food collected by worker ants and change their skin as they grow. This is called molting.

pupae

3. The larvae reach full size after one week or more. They make a hard covering called a cocoon around themselves. At this stage they are called **pupae** (say *pyoo-pee*).

How Do Ants Live?

Ants live together in a group called a colony. Some ants work inside the nest, looking after the queen and her young. Other ants leave the nest to find food.

Worker ants take care of the queen ant.

queen ant

Most ants are female worker ants. There are only a few male ants in a nest. Their job is to help a new queen ant start a new nest.

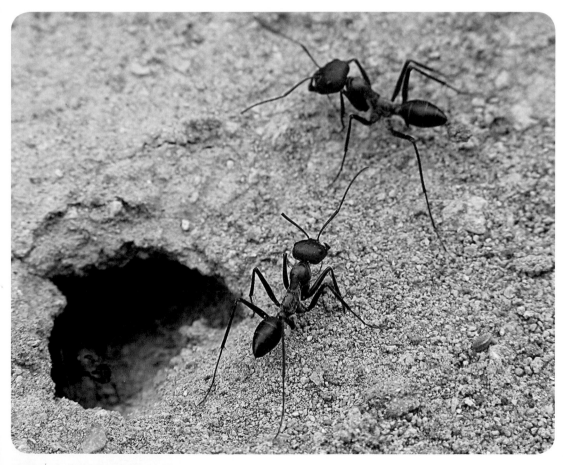

Most of the ants seen outside the nest are female worker ants.

Ant Homes

Ant homes are called nests. They can be small, with just a queen ant and a few worker ants. They can also be very large, with many thousands of worker ants.

A nest is where a queen ant lays her eggs.

eggs

Ant nests are built in the ground, in trees, or in dead wood. A nest can be one small area or lots of rooms deep underground.

Worker ants move larvae and pupae around the nest.

pupae

larvae

Ant Food

Ants only eat liquid food because they cannot chew. They squeeze the liquid out of solid food. Ants love sweet foods such as flower **nectar**.

Ants use their jaws, called mandibles, to pass food into their mouth.

mandibles

When ants find food, they can store it inside a second stomach. Back at the nest, they spit out the food and share it with other ants.

Foods That Ants Eat

Eggs of other insects	
Larvae of other ants	
Flower nectar	
Other insects	
Honey	

How Do Ants Communicate?

Ants use their antennae to communicate with one another. They use special smells on their antennae to tell other ants different things.

Ants rub their antennae against the antennae of other ants to transfer special smells.

Ants can use their antennae to warn other ants of danger. They can also use special smells to mark trails. Other ants can smell these trails and find food.

Ants mark the ground with special smells so other ants can follow their trail.

Threats to the Survival of Ants

Ants are threatened by other animals. Many different **predators** feed on ants. These predators include:

- birds, such as woodpeckers
- **reptiles**, such as lizards
- **mammals**, such as anteaters and armadillos
- other insects, such as ant lion larvae
- other ants.

Ants are an important food for many birds.

Ants from different nests may fight each other, sometimes to the death. They fight over food and to defend their nest.

Ants will fight off other ants that come near their nest.

invading ant

Ants and the Environment

Ants are an important part of the **environment** they live in. Ants feed on other animals and on plants, and many animals feed on them. This is shown in a food web.

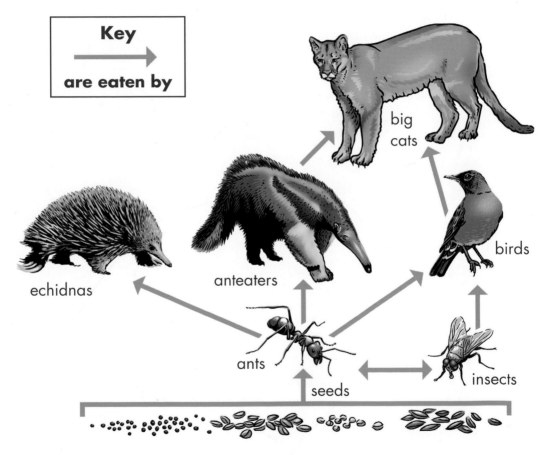

This food web shows what ants eat and what eats them.

Some plants make seeds that ants like to eat. Ants eat part of these seeds. The part that is left over can grow into a new plant.

sticky string

Ponerine ants eat the sticky string of flamingo plant seeds.

Ants and Science

Scientists study ants to see if the local environment is healthy. If the soil has poisons in it, ants will move their nest.

Scientists carefully study ant nests in environments such as rain forests.

The environment is sometimes disturbed by activities such as mining and must be made healthy again. Scientists know the environment is healthy if ants return to the area.

Ants will only build their nests where the environment is healthy.

ant nest

Tips for Watching Ants

These tips will help you watch ants:

- Ants are easier to find in the summer, when they come out in the open more often.
- Look for ants on the ground and under rocks.
- Put out a small amount of food, such as a drop of honey, to attract ants.
- Use a magnifying glass to look at the tiny ant larvae or eggs.

Look but do not touch! Watch ants without touching them to see where they go and what they do.

Be careful when watching ants. Some ants bite!

Glossary

abdomen — The end section of an insect's body.

antennae — Organs found on the heads of insects, used for sensing things.

arachnids — Eight-legged animals, such as spiders, that are part of the arthropod group.

environment — The air, water, and land that surround us.

habitats — Areas in which animals are naturally found.

larvae — The young of an insect.

mammals — Animals that feed their young with their own milk.

mate — Join together to produce young.

nectar — A sweet liquid made by flowers.

predators — Animals that hunt other animals for food.

pupae — What insect larvae turn into before becoming adults.

reptiles — A group of animals with dry, scaly skin.

species — Groups of animals or plants that have similar features.

thorax — The part of the body between the head and abdomen.

Index

A

antennae, 7, 22, 23

B

bees, 5
birds, 24, 26
body parts, 6, 7

C

communication, 7, 22, 23

E

eggs, 14, 18, 21, 30

F

finding ants, 30
flowers, 20, 21
food, 12, 13, 16, 20, 21, 23,
    26, 30
food web, 26

H

habitats, 12, 13
homes, 18, 19

I

insects, 5, 21, 24, 26

L

larvae, 14, 15, 19, 21, 30
life cycles, 14, 15

M

mating, 14

N

nectar, 20, 21
nests, 13, 14, 15, 16, 17, 18,
    19, 21, 25, 27, 28, 29

P

predators, 24
pupae, 15

Q

queen ants, 14, 15, 16, 17, 18

R

rain forests, 13

S

size, 8
smell trails, 23

T

threats to survival, 24, 25

W

wasps, 5
worker ants, 15, 16, 17, 18, 19